Late Elementary Piano Solo

Hazy, Lazy Days

Dennis Alexander

late elementary

Alfred

THE **ALFRED** SIGNATURE SERIES

Hazy, Lazy Days

Dennis Alexander

Andante teneramente

ISBN 0-7390-2414-0

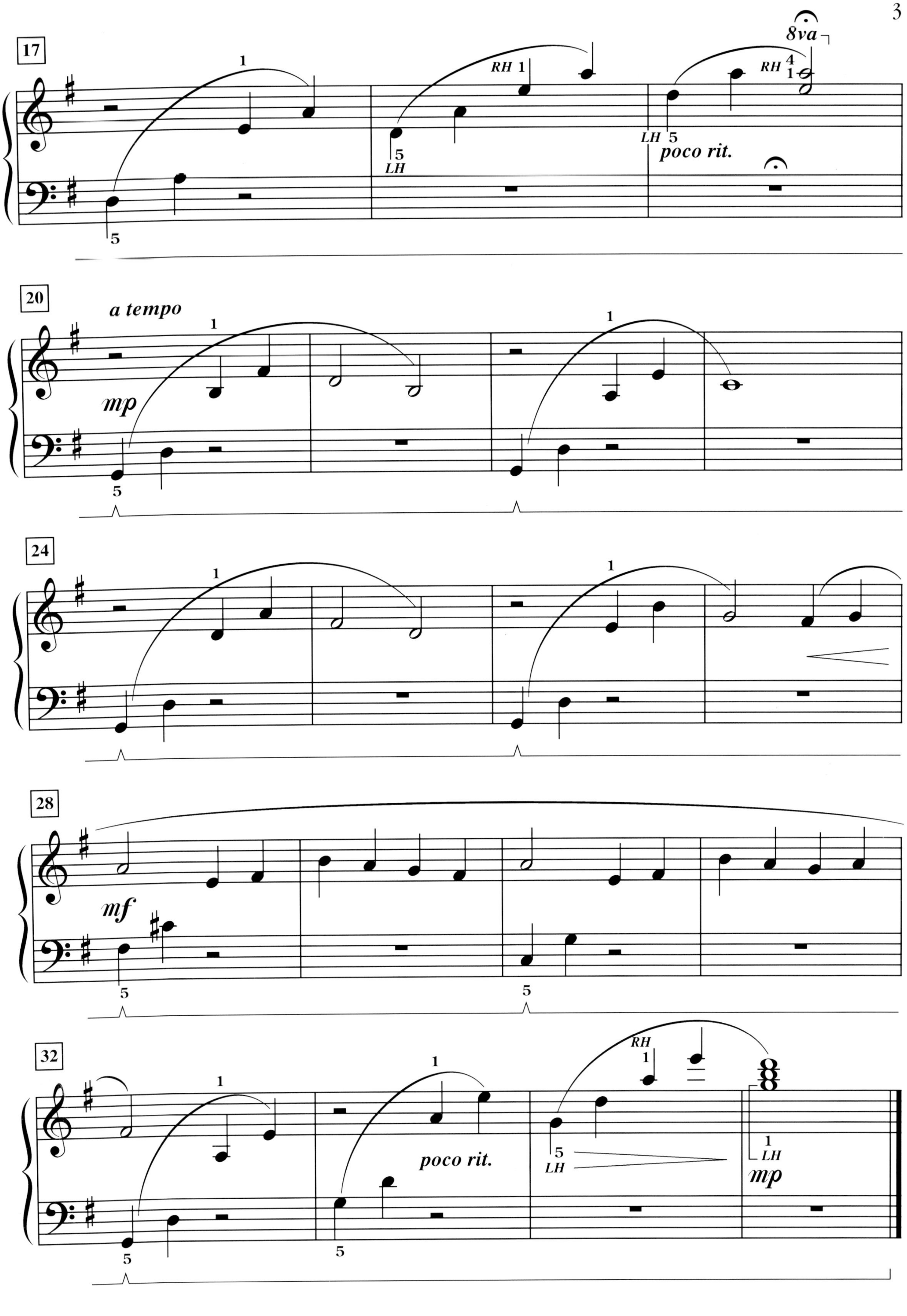
17
8va
RH
LH
poco rit.
20
a tempo
mp
24
28
mf
32
poco rit.
mp

Visit our website!

Search the on-line Catalog

We feature a one-of-a-kind search engine where you can look up specific publications in our catalog by book title, composer, level or even a song title within a book.

Informative and Helpful for **Piano Teachers**

- **Teaching Articles**
  Read special articles written on a variety of subjects pertaining to piano instruction, such as approaches to different styles of music, tips on various teaching methods and more.
- **New Releases**
  Discover what's new even before the music ships to stores.
- **Music Samples**
  Hear previews of music before you buy.
- **Clinic Listings**
  Locate where your favorite Alfred authors will present clinics and workshops.
- **And much more!**
  Find the location of your nearest dealer or learn how to get technical support for your music software. Need more help? E-mail our customer service center (customerservice@alfred.com) and get an answer to virtually any question.

Fun and Educational for **Piano Students**

- **Learn about Your Favorite Alfred Author**
  Read about our composers and see their pictures!
- **Find More Music by Your Favorite Composers**
  Search for additional pieces by your favorite composer by level, title or author.
- **Visit Alfred's Fun Zone**
  Play various music games while learning more about music history and music theory.
- **Other Music Links**
  Find music links that lead you to other fun and interesting sites.

Hazy, Lazy Days • Alexander

Alfred

TP
APEX

9780739024140

Alfred Publishing Co., Inc.
P.O. Box 10003 • 16320 Roscoe Blvd. • Van Nuys, CA 91410-0003
www.alfred.com